A Check-List of the Birds of Idaho

M. Dale Arvey

A Check-list of the Birds of Idaho

By

M. DALE ARVEY

There is comparatively little literature dealing with the avifauna of Idaho, mostly because relatively few persons have done field work in the state. In the ornithological literature, there is nothing even comparable to a "state list," so that when birds supposedly unreported previously from Idaho are found, it is difficult to know whether or not they should be recorded as "new" to the state. The present paper has been prepared in the hope that it will stimulate additions to, and corrections of, the list. It is, admittedly, a beginning.

Material for the present article was obtained from personal collecting in the five years and ten months in which I resided in the state (October, 1938-September, 1944). Also, the published reports that could be found have been drawn upon; these publications are listed in the appended bibliography. Taxonomic problems, of which many are unsolved, are not here considered, since this is merely a list indicating whether or not the species or subspecies, as now understood, is known to be present, whether it is common, and where it might be found.

The nomenclature is that of the Fourth Edition of the American Ornithologists' Union Check-list and its supplements, except where a revision has been made that is seemingly valid but which has not yet been acted upon by the A. O. U. Committee. For each species or subspecies the objective is to give at least one reference to occurrence, as to date and place, as accurately as possible.

Reference is made to southern, central, and northern Idaho. These references denote the Snake River Plains, characterized by sagebrush desert; the wooded regions immediately to the north of this and in the foothills, extending to Idaho County in the west; and the so-called Panhandle, respectively. In all, 292 kinds of birds are recorded in the following list.

LIST OF SPECIES

Gavia immer elasson Bishop. Lesser Loon. Uncommon resident in the lakes of northern Idaho, and generally distributed. Merrill (1897:350) states that the species is common and resident at Fort Sherman.

Gavia stellata (Pontopiddan). Red-throated Loon. Davis (1935b:234) records specimens taken in migration in Minidoka County at the Minidoka Irrigation Project, and Rust (1915:121) states that this species is rare in Kootenai County.

Colymbus grisegena holböllii (Reinhardt). Holboell Grebe. Merrill (1897:349) records this species as common in migration at Fort Sherman.

Colymbus auritus Linnaeus. Horned Grebe. Uncommon resident. Davis (1935b:234) records the bird as a summer visitant at the Minidoka Project.

Colymbus nigricollis californicus (Heermann). Eared Grebe. Fairly common resident along rivers and in lakes. Rust (1915:121) records one specimen taken on Lake Coeur d'Alene in October, 1912.

Aechmophorus occidentalis (Lawrence). Western Grebe. Uncommon resident. Merrill (1897:349) records one specimen from Fort Sherman.

Podilymbus podiceps podiceps (Linnaeus). Pied-billed Grebe. Common resident. Merrill (1897:350) states that it is common at Fort Sherman in the spring and autumn.

Pelecanus erythrorhynchos Gmelin. White Pelican. Resident along the Snake River; large nesting colonies are to be found in Bear Lake County. See Davis (1935b:234) for nesting dates.

Phalacrocorax auritus albociliatus Ridgway. Farallon Cormorant. Davis (1935b:234) records this bird in the Minidoka Project as a regular migrant and gives dates of occurrence. The resident population at the Bear Lake Refuge has been reported as subspecies *auritus* by Behle (1944:68), but probably is *albociliatus*.

Ardea herodias treganzai Court. Treganza Great Blue Heron. Common resident in suitable localities. (Dale Arvey 1505, 7 mi. NE Moscow, Latah County, Idaho, February 19, 1940.)

Leucophoyx thula brewsteri (Thayer and Bangs). Brewster Egret. Davis

5

(1935b:234) records one specimen from the Minidoka Project, taken on September 16, 1919, and Hayward (1934:39) reports the species as breeding at Bear Lake Valley in Bear Lake County.

Nycticorax nycticorax hoactli (Gmelin). Black-crowned Night Heron. Common locally. Hayward (1934:39) reports the bird as resident in Bear Lake Valley.

Botaurus lentiginosus (Montagu). American Bittern. Fairly common resident in suitable localities. Merrill (1897:351) records the American Bittern as rather common at Fort Sherman.

Plegadis mexicana (Gmelin). White-faced Glossy Ibis. Vagrant. Recorded as common at the Minidoka Project by Kenagy (1914:122).

Cygnus columbianus (Ord). Whistling Swan. Resident in the winter in the larger lakes, and transient along the Snake River. (D. A. 1783, 1 mi. S Hagerman, Gooding County, February 1, 1940.)

Cygnus buccinator Richardson. Trumpeter Swan. Merriam (1891:91) states that Bendire found this swan breeding on Henry Lake in 1877, and that two were collected in August of that year. Rust (1915:123) records the species as a rare fall migrant on Lake Coeur d'Alene. There are no recent records.

Branta canadensis (Linnaeus). Canada Goose. Fairly common resident. See Aldrich (1946b) for records of each subspecies.

a. *moffitti* Aldrich. Great Basin Canada Goose. This is the resident race.

b. *occidentalis* (Baird). White-cheeked Goose. Migrant.

c. *leucopareia* (Brandt). Lesser Canada Goose. Migrant.

Branta hutchinsii hutchinsii (Richardson). Hutchins Cackling Goose. Migrant. See Aldrich (1946b) for the status of this goose.

Branta bernicla nigricans (Lawrence). Black Brant. Davis (1935b:234) records this species as a regular migrant in Minidoka County, and indicates that some remain all winter.

Anser albifrons albifrons (Scopoli). White-fronted Goose. Uncommon migrant. Jones (1943:120) records a specimen from "about 10 mi. north Pocatello, Bingham County."

Chen hyperborea hyperborea (Pallas). Lesser Snow Goose. Fairly common transient along the Snake River. Two specimens are in the State Game

Department's mounted collection from the Snake River, probably from near Payette, Payette County.

Chen rossi (Cassin). Ross Goose. Transient along the Snake River. The Game Department collection has two mounted skins from "along the Snake River."

Anas platyryhnchos platyryhnchos Linnaeus. Mallard. Very common resident. (D. A. 1753, Boise River, 1 mi. S Middleton, Canyon County, November 24, 1940.)

Anas acuta tzitzihoa (Vieillot). American Pintail. Resident and common during migration. (D. A. 1752, Snake River, 1 mi. S Hammett, Elmore County, November 16, 1940.)

Anas carolinensis Gmelin. Green-winged Teal. Common resident. (D. A. 1261, Thorn Creek, 7 mi. S Moscow, Latah County, October 30, 1938.)

Anas discors Linnaeus. Blue-winged Teal. Rare resident. Merriam (1891:90) records two shot on Saw Tooth Lake (=Alturas Lake, Blaine County), about October 1.

Anas cyanoptera Vieillot. Cinnamon Teal. Uncommon resident. I observed a female with four young in Bellevue, Blaine County, in July, 1942, and Merrill (1897:350) records a female with young on June 11 at Fort Sherman.

Anas strepera Linnaeus. Gadwall. Resident locally; fairly common in migration. (D. A. 1310, Havenor's, 7 mi. NW Pocatello, Power County, January 2, 1939.)

Mareca americana (Gmelin). Baldpate. Common during migration, and resident along the Snake River. (D. A. 1747, 1 mi. W Bowman Ranch on Boise River, Canyon County, October 26, 1940.)

Spatula clypeata (Linnaeus). Shoveller. Common in migration, and breeds locally. (D. A. 1492, Wallace, Shoshone County, October 22, 1939.)

Aix sponsa (Linnaeus). Wood Duck. Fairly common in migration, and resident locally. Merrill (1897:350) records it as a summer resident at Fort Sherman.

Aythya americana (Eyton). Redhead. Fairly common migrant. Recorded by Merrill (1897:350) at Fort Sherman.

Aythya collaris (Donovan). Ring-necked Duck. Uncommon transient.

7

Merrill (1897:350) records it at Fort Sherman.

Aythya valisineria (Wilson). Canvas-back. Fairly common in migration, and recorded by Low and Nelson (1945:131) as breeding in Bonneville and Caribou counties.

Aythya marila (Linnaeus). Greater Scaup Duck. Fairly common migrant. Davis (1935b:236) records one bird from the Minidoka Project taken on March 28, 1920.

Aythya affinis (Eyton). Lesser Scaup Duck. Common during migration. Davis (1935b:235) lists this bird as a regular winter visitant in Minidoka County from October 30 to May 31.

Glaucionetta clangula americana (Bonaparte). American Golden-eye. Common resident. (D. A. 1476, Bellevue, Blaine County, June 28, 1939.)

Glaucionetta islandica (Gmelin). Barrow Golden-eye. Uncommon transient. Davis (1935b:234) records one specimen taken at the Minidoka Project.

Glaucionetta albeola (Linnaeus). Buffle-head. Common migrant. (D. A. 1852, Snake River, 1 mi. S Hammett, Elmore County, November 15, 1941.)

Histrionicus histrionicus pacificus Brooks. Western Harlequin Duck. Uncommon. Rust (1915:122) records one specimen taken on the marshes of the St. Joseph River in Kootenai County, and Merrill (1897:350) states that it is occasionally taken on the St. Joseph and Coeur d'Alene rivers.

Melanitta fusca subsp.?. White-winged Scoter. Rust (1915:122) records this bird as common on Lake Coeur d'Alene in the winter of 1913.

Melanitta perspicillata (Linnaeus). Surf Scoter. Rust (1915:122) states that this is a rare fall migrant in Kootenai County.

Oxyura jamaicensis rubida (Wilson). Ruddy Duck. Common migrant on the Snake River. Merrill (1897:350) records this duck as "not uncommon in the spring and autumn" at Fort Sherman.

Lophodytes cucullatus (Linnaeus). Hooded Merganser. Common resident in suitable localities. (D. A. 1389, Lewiston, Nezperce County, April 2, 1939.)

Mergus merganser americanus Cassin. American Merganser. Common resident. Merrill (1897:350) states that the bird is common in fall and winter at Fort Sherman.

Mergus serrator Linnaeus. Red-breasted Merganser. Uncommon. Merrill

(1897:350) records one specimen taken "near Fort Sherman."

Cathartes aura teter Friedmann. Western Turkey Vulture. Common resident in southern Idaho, and transient elsewhere. Merrill (1897:352) records it as a summer resident at Fort Sherman.

Accipiter gentilis striatulus (Ridgway). Western Goshawk. Fairly common migrant, and possibly resident. Hand (1933b:36) reports it as resident in northern Idaho. (D. A. 1317, 1318, Nezperce, Lewis County, January 9 and 12, 1939.)

Accipiter striatus velox (Wilson). Sharp-shinned Hawk. Common resident. (D. A. 1296, 4-1/2 mi. NE Genessee, Latah County, November 27, 1938.)

Accipiter cooperii (Bonaparte). Cooper Hawk. Common resident in the forests. (D. A. 1450, Sandpoint, Bonner County, May 24, 1939.)

Buteo jamaicensis calurus Cassin. Western Red-tailed Hawk. Common resident. (D. A. 1352, Moscow, Latah County, March 18, 1939.)

Buteo platypterus platypterus (Vieillot). Broad-winged Hawk. Davis (1936:86) records one specimen of this hawk taken on May 23, 1935, at Castle Creek, 8 mi. S Oreana, Owyhee County.

Buteo swainsoni Bonaparte. Swainson Hawk. Common resident. (D. A. 1451, Moscow, Latah County, May 21, 1939.)

Buteo lagopus s. johannis (Gmelin). American Rough-legged Hawk. Common migrant and possibly resident. (D. A. 1301, 11 mi. SE Genessee, Nezperce County, November 27, 1938.)

Buteo regalis (Gray). Ferruginous Rough-leg. Uncommon migrant. (D. A. 1326, 4 mi. N Minidoka Power Plant, Minidoka County, January 27, 1939.)

Aquila chrysaëtos canadensis (Linnaeus). Golden Eagle. Uncommon resident. Merrill (1897:353) stated that the species occurred "sparingly" at Fort Sherman.

Haliaeetus leucocephalus washingtoniensis (Audubon). Northern Bald Eagle. Uncommon resident in northern Idaho, Merrill (1897:353) stated that a few pairs bred about Lake Coeur d'Alene.

Circus cyaneus hudsonius (Linnaeus). Marsh Hawk. Very common resident. (D. A. 1371, Havenor's, 7 mi. NW Pocatello, Power County, April 1, 1939.)

9

Pandion haliaetus carolinensis (Gmelin). Osprey. Uncommon resident. Merrill (1897:353) reported the bird as frequent in the summer at Fort Sherman.

Falco mexicanus Schlegel. Prairie Falcon. Fairly common resident. (D. A. 1319, American Falls, Bingham County, January 16, 1939.)

Falco peregrinus anatum Bonaparte. Duck Hawk. Uncommon resident. Bond (1946:104) lists this bird as a rare breeder in Idaho.

Falco columbarius bendirei Swann. Western Pigeon Hawk. Rust (1915:124) records one specimen from Coeur d'Alene as subspecies *columbarius*; although the skin has not been checked by me, it would seem to be more likely of subspecies *bendirei*, corresponding to others taken in northern Idaho.

Falco sparverius sparverius Linnaeus. Eastern Sparrow Hawk. Common resident. (D. A. 1267, Little Bear Ridge, 5 mi. SW Troy, Latah County, November 2, 1939.)

Dendragapus obscurus (Say). Blue Grouse. Common resident.

a. *obscurus* (Say). Dusky Grouse. Specimens from southeastern Idaho are referable to this race.

b. *richardsonii* (Douglas). Richardson Grouse. This is the resident race of southwestern Idaho north to Idaho County, where intergradation occurs with the next form. (D. A. 1431, 1432, 10 mi. SW Riggins, Idaho County, May 14, 1939.)

c. *pallidus* Swarth. Oregon Dusky Grouse. Birds in the northern portion of the state are of this race.

Canachites franklinii (Douglas). Franklin Grouse. Uncommon resident. I have observed the birds in the Selway National Forest, in Idaho County, and specimens have been taken in Bonner County. (D. A. 1336, 1337, 6 mi. S Coolin, Bonner County, February 19, 1939.)

Bonasa umbellus (Linnaeus). Ruffed Grouse. Common resident. See Aldrich and Friedman (1943) for ranges of the following races.

a. *phaia* Aldrich and Friedmann. Idaho Ruffed Grouse. This is the race resident in southwestern Idaho, and it intergrades with the two following forms.

b. *umbelloides* (Douglas). Gray Ruffed Grouse. Resident in northern

Idaho.

c. *incanus* Aldrich and Friedmann. Hoary Ruffed Grouse. Resident in southeastern Idaho.

Lagopus leucurus altipetens Osgood. Southern White-tailed Ptarmigan. Several specimens of this bird are mounted in a collection in Idaho City, having been collected "in the vicinity."

Pedioecetes phasianellus columbianus (Ord). Columbian Sharp-tailed Grouse. One specimen was sent me from Bonner County, where the species was said to be fairly abundant. (D. A. 1513, 15 mi. N Priest River, Bonner County, April 1, 1940.)

Centrocercus urophasianus (Bonaparte). Sage Grouse. Common locally. Previously numerous, and now recovering from a severe decline in numbers. Merriam (1891:93) speaks of using these birds for fresh meat during much of his trip.

Perdix perdix perdix (Linnaeus). European Partridge. Common since its introduction.

Colinus virginianus texanus (Lawrence). Texas Bob-white. Common resident in southern Idaho. Merriam (1891:92) states that the birds were first introduced at Boise, Ada County.

Lophortyx californica brunnescens Ridgway. California Quail. Introduced into southern Idaho; not numerous but establishing itself in the foothills.

Oreortyx picta picta (Douglas). Plumed Quail. Common resident. Wyman (1912c:538) states that this species was not present in Idaho prior to about 1900, having at that time extended its range from Oregon.

Phasianus colchicus Linnaeus. Ring-necked Pheasant. Common resident since its introduction; there is considerable admixture of races in the stock.

Grus canadensis tabida (Peters). Sandhill Crane. Uncommon resident. Merriam (1891:91) reports the bird breeding near Fort Lapwai, Nezperce County, in June 1871, and Davis (1935b:234) states that it is a regular migrant at the Minidoka Project.

Rallus limicola limicola Vieillot. Virginia Rail. Davis (1923) states that this rail is uncommon at the Minidoka Project, but that it was abundant in earlier years.

11

Porzana carolina (Linnaeus). Sora. Uncommon resident. Merriam (1891:91) recorded this species from Big Lost River, "about 8 mi. above Arco," Butte County, on July 26.

Fulica americana Gmelin. American Coot. Common resident. (D. A. 1745, Notus, Canyon County, October 20, 1940.)

Charadrius vociferus vociferus Linnaeus. Killdeer. Common resident in the Transition Life-zone. Rust (1915:123) records the earliest arrival date for the bird in Kootenai County as March 9, 1913, and says that it leaves by September 1.

Pluvialis dominica fulva (Gmelin). Pacific Golden Plover. Sloanaker (1925:73) records one specimen of this bird, shot from a flock of four near Coeur d'Alene on Lake Chactolet on October 1, 1923.

Squatarola squatarola (Linnaeus). Black-bellied Plover. Rust (1915:123) records one specimen of this bird taken on the St. Joseph marshes, Kootenai County.

Capella gallinago delicata (Ord). Wilson Snipe. Fairly common resident. (D. A. 1739, Boise River, 3 mi. W Boise, Ada County, October 17, 1940.)

Numenius americanus Bechstein. Long-billed Curlew. Uncommon resident. See Oberholser (1918) for ranges of the following subspecies.

a. *americanus* Bechstein. Long-billed Curlew. Resident in southern Idaho.

b. *parvus* Bishop. Northern Curlew. The resident population in northern Idaho is referable to this subspecies.

Actitis macularia (Linnaeus). Spotted Sandpiper. Common resident in the Canadian Life-zone. (D. A. 1807, junction of Simmon's Cr. and Boise River, Boise County, July 5, 1941.)

Tringa solitaria cinnamomea (Brewster). Western Solitary Sandpiper. Davis (1935b:236) took one specimen on April 9, 1920 at the Minidoka Project, and records the bird as erratic in occurrence.

Catoptrophorus semipalmatus inornatus (Brewster). Western Willet. Davis (1935b:235) records this bird as a summer visitant at the Minidoka Project, and gives dates of its occurrence there.

Totanus melanoleucus (Gmelin). Greater Yellow-legs. Davis (1935b:234) records this bird at the Minidoka Project in migration.

Totanus flavipes (Gmelin). Lesser Yellow-legs. Fairly common in migration. (D. A. 1742, Notus, Canyon County, October 20, 1940.)

Erolia melanotos (Vieillot). Pectoral Sandpiper. Merrill (1897:351) records this bird as common in 1896 from August to October at Fort Sherman, and a number of specimens were taken.

Erolia minutilla (Vieillot). Least Sandpiper. Fairly common migrant. Davis (1935b:234) gives dates of migration of this bird at the Minidoka Project.

Limnodromus griseus scolopaceus (Say). Long-billed Dowitcher. Merrill (1897:351) collected five specimens on September 12 on the St. Joseph marshes.

Micropalama himantopus (Bonaparte). Stilt Sandpiper. Davis (1935b:234) collected one bird at the Minidoka Project on May 13, 1919, and stated that the species was erratic in occurrence.

Ereunetes mauri Cabanis. Western Sandpiper. Rust (1917:32) recorded this bird on August 27 near Spencer, Fremont County, and also at Henry Lake.

Limosa fedoa (Linnaeus). Marbled Godwit. Davis (1935b:236) records one specimen taken on August 1, 1920, at the Minidoka Project.

Limosa haemastica (Linnaeus). Hudsonian Godwit. Davis (1935b:236) records one bird taken at the Minidoka Project on July 7, 1919.

Crocethia alba (Pallas). Sanderling. Davis (1935b:236) records this bird from the Minidoka Project in migration, and he took one specimen on May 19, 1921.

Recurvirostra americana Gmelin. Avocet. Uncommon resident in southern Idaho. (D. A. 1631, Snake River at Hagerman, Gooding County, June 16, 1940.)

Himantopus mexicanus (Müller). Black-necked Stilt. Davis (1935b:235) records this bird from Minidoka as a summer visitant, and gives dates of its occurrence.

Phalaropus fulicarius (Linnaeus). Red Phalarope. Hand (1935:180) reports one bird of this species in October on the St. Joseph River at St. Maries, Benewah County.

Steganopus tricolor Vieillot. Wilson Phalarope. Uncommon. Davis

13

(1935b:236) took one specimen at the Minidoka Project on May 13, 1919.

Lobipes lobatus (Linnaeus). Northern Phalarope. Uncommon resident. Davis (1935b:236) reports the species as erratic at the Minidoka Project, where he took one specimen on May 13, 1919.

Stercorarius pomarinus (Temminck). Pomarine Jaeger. Davis (1935b:236) took one bird "on the Snake River," on September 4, 1919.

Larus argentatus thayeri Brooks. Thayer Gull. Merrill (1897:350) records several birds of this species taken in the fall and winter on Lake Coeur d'Alene.

Larus californicus Lawrence. California Gull. Common in the winter, and possibly breeds along the Snake River. Davis (1935b:235) records this bird as a common summer visitant at the Minidoka Project.

Larus delawarensis Ord. Ring-billed Gull. Uncommon straggler. Merrill (1897:350) records it in the winter at Fort Sherman.

Larus pipixcan Wagler. Franklin Gull. Late winter and spring straggler. See Slipp (1942).

Larus philadelphia (Ord). Bonaparte Gull. This gull is recorded by Merrill (1897:350) as taken at Fort Sherman in November.

Sterna forsteri Nuttall. Forster Tern. Davis (1935b:235) lists this bird as a summer visitant in Minidoka County, and gives dates of its occurrence there.

Sterna hirundo hirundo Linnaeus. Common Tern. Rust (1915:121) states that this tern is rare in Kootenai County.

Hydroprogne caspia (Pallas). Caspian Tern. Common during migration. Davis (1935b:234) records the species as common in migration at the Minidoka Project, and gives dates of its occurrence.

Chlidonias nigra surinamensis (Gmelin). Black Tern. Fairly common on lakes; evidently resident. Rust (1915:121) records this bird as common in June, 1914, on the St. Joseph Marshes.

Columba fasciata fasciata Say. Band-tailed Pigeon. Rare at present. Merrill (1897:349) states that Cooper listed this bird in what is now Idaho.

Zenaidura macroura marginella (Woodhouse). Western Mourning Dove. Common summer resident, frequently remaining in winter. Rust (1915:123) lists the bird as a fairly common summer resident in Kootenai County.

14

Ectopistes migratorius (Linnaeus). Passenger Pigeon. Extinct. Merrill (1897:349) states that Cooper listed this species from Montana and from what is now Idaho.

Coccyzus americanus occidentalis Ridgway. California Cuckoo. This bird was reported by Davis (1935b:236), as taken May 16, 1918 at the Minidoka Project, and he says that nests have been taken near Rupert by Kenagy.

Coccyzus erythropthalmus (Wilson). Black-billed Cuckoo. One breeding bird of this species was reported by Arvey (1941:291), taken at Slide Gulch on the Boise River, Boise County, on July 10, 1941. Since this time I have observed the bird twice in Boise, Ada County, in the summer.

Tyto alba pratincola (Bonaparte). Barn Owl. Uncommon resident. One specimen in the University of Idaho collection of mounted birds was taken near Moscow, Latah County.

Otus asio (Linnaeus). Screech Owl. Common resident.

a. *macfarlanei* (Brewster). MacFarlane Screech Owl. Resident in southern Idaho. (D. A. 1861, Boise, Ada County, April 11, 1942.)

b. *brewsteri* Ridgway. Brewster Screech Owl. Resident in northern Idaho. (D. A. 1312, Lapwai, Nezperce County, December 25, 1938.)

Otus flammeolus flammeolus (Kaup). Flammulated Screech Owl. Rare resident. Specimens have been taken in two localities. Merriam (1891:96) took one specimen on the west side of Big Wood River, "only a few miles north of Ketchum, September 22," 1890. The record from Blaine County and the one of Rust (1915:125), near Fernan Lake, September 28, 1914, are the only two positive records of this species to my knowledge.

Bubo virginianus (Gmelin). Great Horned Owl. Common resident. See A. O. U. Check-list (1931).

a. *wapacuthu* (Gmelin). Arctic Horned Owl. Migrant.

b. *occidentalis* Stone. Montana Horned Owl. Resident in central and southeastern Idaho.

c. *lagophonus* (Oberholser). Northwestern Horned Owl. Resident in western and northern Idaho. (D. A. 1486, 10 mi. SW Riggins, Idaho County, September 15, 1939.)

Nyctea scandiaca (Linnaeus). Snowy Owl. Casual migrant. Merrill (1897:352) stated that there was an invasion of owls of this species in the winter of 1896-'97, and many were observed during that time at Fort Sherman.

Surnia ulula caparoch (Müller). American Hawk Owl. Uncommon. Hand (1933a:32) reports one specimen of this owl taken at Stanley Butte, 10 mi. S Lochsa River, Idaho County, on November 3, 1925, and mentions one other observed in the summer. He suggests that the bird breeds in northern Idaho.

Glaucidium gnoma californicum Sclater. California Pygmy Owl. Fairly common resident in the Canadian Life-zone. Specimens seem referable to subspecies *pinicola*, recently synonymized by the A. O. U. Committee. (D. A. 1311, Priest River, Bonner County, January 3, 1939.)

Speotyto cunicularia hypugaea (Bonaparte). Western Burrowing Owl. Fairly common local resident. (D. A. 1388, 10 mi. W Boise, Ada County, April 2, 1939.)

Strix nebulosa nebulosa Forster. Great Gray Owl. Vagrant. A specimen, D. A. 1303, taken on December 8, 1938, was sent me from 9 mi. NE Grangeville, Idaho County, December 8, 1938.

Asio otus wilsonianus (Lesson). Long-eared Owl. Fairly common resident. (D. A. 1532, 5 mi. SW Moscow, Latah County, April 29, 1940.)

Asio flammeus flammeus (Pontoppidan). Short-eared Owl. Very common resident in the Transition Life-zone. (D. A. 1346, 2 mi. S Moscow, Latah County, March 7, 1939.)

Aegolius funereus richardsoni (Bonaparte). Richardson Owl. Rust (1915:125) records this bird as a rare winter visitor in Kootenai County, and Merrill (1897:353) lists two specimens taken "early in the spring of 1894 ... about seven miles from the fort."

Aegolius acadicus acadicus (Gmelin). Saw-whet Owl. Rare. Davis (1935b:235) says that this is a regular winter visitor at the Minidoka Project, and Merrill (1897:353) lists one specimen taken at Fort Sherman, on January 19.

Phalaenoptilus nuttallii nuttallii (Audubon). Nuttall Poorwill. Uncommon resident. Merriam (1891:98) records this species from "the lava beds west of Blackfoot" on July 17, 1872.

Chordeiles minor hesperis Grinnell. Pacific Nighthawk. Common resident in the Transition Life-zone. (D. A. 1468, 2 mi. S Hailey, on Wood River, Blaine County, June 25, 1939.)

Chaetura vauxi vauxi (Townsend). Vaux Swift. Merrill (1897:354) reports this bird as resident at Fort Sherman, as does Burleigh (1923:658) at Clark's Fork, Bonner County.

Aëronautes saxatalis saxatalis (Woodhouse). White-throated Swift. Fairly common resident in suitable localities. The Museum of Vertebrate Zoölogy has one specimen of this bird taken on Salmon Creek, 8 mi. W Rogerson, Twin Falls County.

Archilochus alexandri (Boucier and Mulsant). Black-chinned Hummingbird. Rust (1915:125) records this species as resident in Kootenai County.

Selasphorus platycercus platycercus (Swainson). Broad-tailed Hummingbird. Common resident in southern Idaho. Davis (1935b:236) states that the bird is of erratic occurrence at the Minidoka Project.

Selasphorus rufus (Gmelin). Rufous Hummingbird. Fairly common resident. Merrill (1897:355) states that this species is common in spring at Fort Sherman.

Stellula calliope (Gould). Calliope Hummingbird. Common resident. (D. A. 1541, 10 mi. NE Moscow, Latah County, May 10, 1940.)

Megaceryle alcyon caurina (Grinnell). Western Belted Kingfisher. Common resident in suitable localities. (D. A. 1518, 7 mi. NE Moscow, Latah County, April 19, 1940.)

Colaptes cafer (Gmelin). Red-shafted Flicker. Common resident.

a. *collaris* Vigors. Red-shafted Flicker. Resident in southwestern and northern Idaho. Many specimens show yellow remiges and rectrices, and are perhaps hybrids with the species *auratus*. (D. A. 1731, Owl Creek, in Blaine County, September 8, 1940.)

b. *canescens* Brodkorb. Red-shafted Flicker. Resident in southeastern Idaho. See Brodkorb (1935a:1).

Hylatomus pileatus picinus (Bangs). Western Pileated Woodpecker. Fairly common resident in the Transition Life-zone. (D. A. 1498, 10 mi. NE Moscow, Latah County, November 18, 1939.)

Asyndesmus lewis Gray. Lewis Woodpecker. Common resident. Merrill

17

(1897:354) records this bird as common "around Fort Sherman."

Sphyrapicus varius nuchalis Baird. Red-naped Sapsucker. Fairly common resident. (D. A. 1485, 10 mi. SW Riggins, Idaho County, September 15, 1939.)

Sphyrapicus thyroideus thyroideus (Cassin). Williamson Sapsucker. Uncommon resident. The Museum of Vertebrate Zoölogy has one specimen taken on the W rim Copenhagen Basin, 8400 ft., Wasatch Mountains, Bear Lake County.

Dendrocopos villosus monticola Anthony. Rocky Mountain Hairy Woodpecker. Common resident. (D. A. 1662, 4 mi. NW Pollock, Idaho County, July 1, 1940.)

Dendrocopos pubescens leucurus (Hartlaub). Batchelder Woodpecker. Common resident. (D. A. 1495, Potlatch, Latah County, November 3, 1939.)

Dendrocopos albolarvatus albolarvatus (Cassin). Northern White-headed Woodpecker. Uncommon resident. (D. A. 1434, 10 mi. SW Riggins, Idaho County, May 14, 1939.)

Picoïdes arcticus (Swainson). Arctic Three-toed Woodpecker. Uncommon resident in northern Idaho. Merrill (1897:354) reports these birds as resident at Fort Sherman.

Picoïdes tridactylus (Linnaeus). Uncommon resident.

a. *dorsalis* Baird. Alpine Three-toed Woodpecker. Resident in southern Idaho; the Museum of Vertebrate Zoölogy has specimens taken at W rim Copenhagen Basin, 8400 ft., Wasatch Mountains, Bear Lake County.

b. *fasciatus* Baird. Alaska Three-toed Woodpecker. Resident in northern Idaho. There are specimens in the Museum of Vertebrate Zoölogy taken at Coolin, Priest Lake, Kootenai County.

Tyrannus tyrannus (Linnaeus). Eastern Kingbird. Common resident in northern Idaho; casual in southern portion. (Univ. Idaho, No. 39, Moscow, Latah County, May 19, 1937.)

Tyrannus verticalis Say. Arkansas Kingbird. Common resident in southern Idaho. (D. A. 1794, Arrowrock Reservoir, Boise County, June 15, 1941.)

Myiarchus cinerascens cinerascens (Lawrence). Ash-throated Flycatcher. Uncommon resident in southern Idaho. (D. A. 1837, Head Taylor Creek,

18

Boise National Forest, Boise County, August 7, 1941.)

Sayornis saya saya (Bonaparte). Say Phoebe. Fairly common resident in southern Idaho. (D. A. 1720, 4 mi. NW Pollock, Idaho County.)

Empidonax traillii brewsteri Oberholser. Little Flycatcher. Fairly common resident in the Transition Life-zone. (Univ. Idaho No. 121, Moscow Mountain, Latah County, June 15, 1938.)

Empidonax hammondii (Xantus). Hammond Flycatcher. Uncommon resident in the Transition Life-zone. (Univ. Idaho No. 62, Avery, Latah County, July 10, 1937.)

Empidonax wrightii Baird. Wright Flycatcher. Common resident in the Transition Life-zone. (D. A. 1560, Robinson's Lake, 10 mi. E Moscow, Latah County, May 16, 1940.)

Empidonax griseus Brewster. Gray Flycatcher. Davis (1934) records one specimen of this species taken June 3, 1934, at Riddle, Owyhee County.

Contopus richardsonii richardsonii (Swainson). Western Wood Pewee. Common resident. (D. A. 1617, 9 mi. ESE Moscow, Latah County, June 5, 1940.)

Nuttallornis borealis (Swainson). Olive-sided Flycatcher. Uncommon resident. (D. A. 1786, Idaho City, Boise County, May 23, 1941.)

Eremophila alpestris (Linnaeus). Horned Lark. Common resident. See Behle (1942) for ranges of the following races.

a. *lamprochroma* Oberholser. Oregon Horned Lark. Southwestern Idaho, and intergrading with the next two races.

b. *utahensis* Behle. Great Salt Lake Horned Lark. Resident in central and southeastern Idaho.

c. *merrilli* Dwight. Dusky Horned Lark. Northern Idaho.

Tachycineta thalassina lepida Mearns. Violet-green Swallow. Common resident. (D. A. 1654, 4 mi. NW Pollock, Idaho County, June 27, 1940.)

Iridoprocne bicolor (Vieillot). Tree Swallow. Fairly common resident. Burleigh (1923:655) records the birds at Clark's Fork, Bonner County.

Riparia riparia riparia (Linnaeus). Bank Swallow. Fairly common resident in suitable localities. (D. A. 1453, 4-1/2 mi. SW Moscow, Latah County, May 26, 1939.)

Stelgidopteryx ruficollis serripennis (Audubon). Rough-winged Swallow.

Low (1945:132) records a colony of these birds and Bank Swallows nesting together at Gray's Lake, in Caribou County.

Hirundo rustica erythrogaster Boddaert. Barn Swallow. Common resident. (D. A. 1420, Troy, Latah County, May 6, 1939.)

Petrochelidon pyrronota albifrons (Rafinesque). Northern Cliff Swallow. Common resident. (D. A. 1415, Troy, Latah County, May 6, 1939.)

Perisoreus canadensis bicolor A. H. Miller. Idaho Jay. Common resident in central and northern Idaho. (D. A. 1344, Blue Creek, 8 mi. NE Priest Lake, Bonner County, March 5, 1939.)

Cyanocitta stelleri annectens (Baird). Black-headed Jay. Common resident. (D. A. 1257, Moscow Mountain, Latah County, October 25, 1938.)

Aphelocoma coerulescens woodhousei (Baird). Woodhouse Jay. Uncommon resident in southern Idaho. The A. O. U. Check-list records this species from southern Idaho; it is resident in the piñon-juniper association.

Pica pica hudsonia (Sabine). American Magpie. Common resident. (D. A. 1782, Star, Canyon County, May 1, 1940.)

Corvus corax sinuatus Wagler. American Raven. Common resident in southern Idaho. Davis (1935b:235) lists the bird as a regular winter visitant at the Minidoka Project.

Corvus brachyrynchos hesperis Ridgway. Western Crow. Common resident. Davis (1935b:235) lists the bird as a winter visitant at the Minidoka Project.

Gymnorhinus cyanocephalus Wied. Piñon Jay. Resident locally in piñon-juniper association. Davis (1935b:235) states that this is a regular winter visitant in Minidoka County.

Nucifraga columbiana (Wilson). Clark Nutcracker. Common resident of forested areas of central and northern Idaho. See Burleigh (1923:655).

Parus atricapillus Linnaeus. Black-capped Chickadee. Very common resident. See Duvall (1945) for ranges of the following races.

a. *septentrionalis* Harris. Long-tailed Chickadee. Resident in eastern Idaho; intergrades with the next two races.

b. *nevadensis* (Linsdale). Pallid Black-capped Chickadee. Resident in southwestern and south-central Idaho.

c. *fortuitus* (Davison and Bowles). Columbian Black-capped

Chickadee. Resident in northern and central Idaho.

Parus gambeli Ridgway. Mountain Chickadee. Common resident in the Transition Life-zone.

a. *grinnelli* (van Rossem). Grinnell Chickadee. Resident in central and northern Idaho. (D. A. 1508, 10 mi. ESE Moscow, Latah County, March 18, 1940.)

b. *inyoensis* (Grinnell). Inyo Chickadee. Resident in southeastern Idaho. (D. A. 1361, Havenor's, 7 mi. NW Pocatello, Power County, April 1, 1939.)

Parus rufescens rufescens Townsend. Chestnut-backed Chickadee. Resident in central and northern Idaho. Rust (1915:129) records the bird from Fernan Lake, Kootenai County.

Parus inornatus griseus (Ridgway). Gray Titmouse. Fairly common resident in southeastern Idaho in the piñon-juniper association. (D. A. 1366, Pocatello Creek, 3 mi. E Pocatello, Bannock County, April 2, 1939.)

Psaltriparus minimus plumbeus (Baird). Lead-colored Bush-tit. Uncommon resident in the piñon-juniper association of southern Idaho. The Museum of Vertebrate Zoölogy has specimens collected by me at S Fork Owyhee River, 12 mi. N Nevada line, Owyhee County.

Sitta carolinensis tenuissima Grinnell. Inyo Nuthatch. Fairly common resident in the Transition Life-zone. (D. A. 1286, 3 mi. NE Princeton, Latah County, November 20, 1938.)

Sitta canadensis Linnaeus. Red-breasted Nuthatch. Common resident in the Transition Life-zone. (D. A. 1905, 11 mi. SSW Idaho City, Boise County, October 20, 1946.)

Sitta pygmaea melanotis van Rossem. Black-eared Nuthatch. Fairly common resident in the Transition Life-zone. (D. A. 1552, 10 mi. NE Moscow, Latah County, May 11, 1940.)

Certhia familiaris caurina Aldrich. Northwestern Creeper. Common resident in the Transition Life-zone. (D. A. 1304, Paradise Ridge, 3 mi. S Moscow, Latah County, December 10, 1938.)

Cinclus mexicanus unicolor Bonaparte. Dipper. Common resident. Rust (1915:128) reports that this bird is regularly seen along mountain streams in Kootenai County.

Troglodytes aëdon parkmanii Audubon. Western House Wren. Common resident. (Univ. Idaho No. 50, Moscow, Latah County, May 25, 1937.)

Troglodytes troglodytes pacificus Baird. Western Winter Wren. Uncommon resident in the Canadian Life-zone of central and northern Idaho. (D. A. 1269, Lochsa River, at Van Camp, Idaho County, November 5, 1939.)

Telmatodytes palustris pulverius Aldrich. Northwestern Long-billed Marsh Wren. Common resident in suitable localities. (D. A. 1769, 2 mi. SW Notus, Canyon County, February 20, 1941.)

Catherpes mexicanus griseus Aldrich. Northern Canyon Wren. Uncommon resident in southern Idaho, extending north at least to Idaho County. (D. A. 1702, 4 mi. NW Pollock, Idaho County, July 15, 1940.)

Salpinctes obsoletus obsoletus (Say). Common Rock Wren. Resident in southern Idaho. (D. A. 1799, Boise, Ada County, June 24, 1941.)

Dumetella carolinensis ruficrissa Aldrich. Western Catbird. Common resident in northern Idaho, and possibly in the southern portion of the state. (D. A. 1467, 2 mi. NE Moscow, Latah County, June 2, 1939.)

Oreoscoptes montanus (Townsend). Sage Thrasher. Resident in the sagebrush area from Idaho County south. (D. A. 1645, 4 mi. NW Pollock, Idaho County, June 25, 1940.)

Turdus migratorius Linnaeus. Robin. Common resident in the Transition Life-zone.

a. *caurinus* (Grinnell). Northwestern Robin. Common migrant. (Univ. Idaho No. 216, Moscow, Latah County, August 25, 1937.)

b. *propinquus* Ridgway. Western Robin. Resident. (D. A. 1893, Boise, Ada County, May 1, 1944.)

Ixoreus naevius meruloides (Swainson). Northern Varied Thrush. Uncommon resident in the Transition Life-zone. (D. A. 1231, Moscow, Latah County, October 7, 1938.)

Hylocichla guttata (Pallas). Hermit Thrush. Fairly common resident.

a. *guttata* (Pallas). Alaska Hermit Thrush. The A. O. U. Check-list (1931) states that these birds migrate through Idaho.

b. *auduboni* (Baird). Audubon Hermit Thrush. Resident. (D. A. 1230, Moscow, Latah County, October 1, 1938.)

Hylocichla ustulata almae Oberholser. Western Olive-backed Thrush. Fairly common resident. (D. A. 1616, 9 mi. ESE Moscow, Latah County, June 5, 1940.)

Hylocichla fuscescens salicicola Ridgway. Willow Thrush. Fairly common resident. The Museum of Vertebrate Zoölogy has specimens of this species, taken at Castle Creek Ranger Station, Idaho County, 7 mi. SE Murphy, Owyhee County, and 3 mi. W Swan Valley, Bonneville County.

Sialia mexicanus occidentalis Townsend. Western Bluebird. Resident in northern Idaho. Rust (1915:129) states that the species is fairly common at Coeur d'Alene Lake.

Sialia currucoides (Bechstein). Mountain Bluebird. Very common resident. (D. A. 1789, Black Creek, 12 mi. SE Boise, Ada County, March 7, 1941.)

Myadestes townsendi (Audubon). Townsend Solitaire. Uncommon resident in the boreal zones. (D. A. 1294, 7 mi. E Genessee, Latah County, November 27, 1938.)

Polioptila caerulea amoenissima Grinnell. Western Gnatcatcher. Brodkorb (1935b:312) records one specimen of this bird taken at 6,000 ft. "about eight miles southwest of Raymond, Bear Lake County," on October 7, 1932.

Regulus satrapa olivaceus Baird. Western Golden-crowned Kinglet. Resident; fairly common in winter. (D. A. 1229, Moscow, Latah County, October 1, 1938.)

Regulus calendula cineraceus Grinnell. Western Ruby-crowned Kinglet. Resident; one of the most common winter birds. (D. A. 1902, Cottonwood Creek, 5 mi. NNE Boise, Ada County, October 5, 1946.)

Anthus spinoletta pacificus Todd. Western Pipit. Common migrant. (D. A. 1849, Black Creek Reservoir, 12 mi. SE Boise, Ada County, October 11, 1941.)

Bombycilla garrulus pallidiceps Reichenow. Bohemian Waxwing. Common sporadically in winter. Taylor (1918:226) reported this bird breeding near Sandpoint, Bonner County.

Bombycilla cedrorum Vieillot. Cedar Waxwing. Very common in winter, often with the preceding species; resident in Kootenai and Bonner counties, and probably elsewhere in the State. Rust (1915:128) records a nest with three fresh eggs on June 28 at Fernan Creek, Kootenai County.

Lanius excubitor invictus Grinnell. Northwestern Shrike. Casual migrant. (D. A. 1875, Boise, Ada County, February 3, 1943.)

Lanius ludovicianus gambeli Ridgway. California Shrike. Miller (1931:79) states that the resident population of this species is referred to this race. Common resident in the Sonoran zones.

Sturnus vulgaris Linnaeus. Starling. These birds have been reported for several years; specimens were first reported by Jones (1946:142) from Bannock County.

Vireo huttoni huttoni Cassin. Hutton Vireo. Very common resident in the Transition Life-zone. (D. A. 1413, Troy, Latah County, May 6, 1939.)

Vireo solitarius cassinii Xantus. Cassin Vireo. Common resident in the Transition Life-zone. The Museum of Vertebrate Zoölogy has a specimen taken 3 mi. W Payette Lake, Adams County.

Vireo olivaceus (Linnaeus). Red-eyed Vireo. Common resident. The Museum of Vertebrate Zoölogy has a specimen of this vireo taken 4 mi. W Meadow Creek, Idaho County.

Vireo gilvus swainsonii Baird. Western Warbling Vireo. Very common resident. (Univ. Idaho No. 119, Moscow, Latah County, June 14, 1938.)

Vermivora celata orestera Oberholser. Rocky Mountain Orange-crowned Warbler. Common resident. (Univ. Idaho No. 204, Moscow, Latah County, August 16, 1938.)

Vermivora ruficapilla ridgwayi van Rossem. Calaveras Warbler. Burleigh (1923:662) states that this warbler is fairly common at Clark's Fork, Bonner County, in July and August.

Dendroica petechia morcomi Coale. Rocky Mountain Yellow Warbler. Very common resident. (Univ. Idaho No. 175, Moscow Mountain, Latah County, July 29, 1938.)

Dendroica auduboni auduboni (Townsend). Audubon Warbler. Common resident. (D. A. 1555, 10 mi. NE Moscow, Latah County, May 11, 1940.)

Dendroica nigrescens (Townsend). Black-throated Gray Warbler. Fairly common in migration, and probably resident. The Museum of Vertebrate Zoölogy has a specimen taken at Indian Creek, 12 mi. SE Riddle, Owyhee County.

Dendroica townsendi (Townsend). Townsend Warbler. Fairly common in migration. Burleigh (1923:663) states that the bird is resident at Clark's Fork, Bonner County.

Seiurus noveboracensis notabilis Ridgway. Grinnell Water-thrush. Merrill (1897:349) records this bird from the State.

Oporornis tolmiei (Townsend). Macgillivray Warbler. Common resident. (D. A. 1421, Troy, Latah County, May 6, 1939.)

Geothlypis trichas occidentalis Brewster. Western Yellow-throat. Common resident in suitable localities. (D. A. 1863, 2 mi. W Boise, Ada County, May 8, 1942.)

Icteria virens auricollis (Lichtenstein). Long-tailed Chat. Common resident. (D. A. 1800, Cinch Creek, Arrowrock Reservoir, Boise County, June 28, 1941.)

Wilsonia pusilla pileolata (Pallas). Northern Pileolated Warbler. Burleigh (1923:663) records this bird as a common resident at Clark's Fork, Bonner County; uncommon in southern Idaho.

Setophaga ruticilla (Linnaeus). American Redstart. There are some records of casual visitants in southern Idaho, and Burleigh (1923:663) states that it is a summer resident at Clark's Fork, Bonner County.

Passer domesticus (Linnaeus). English Sparrow. This cosmopolitan bird can be found wherever there is a human habitation.

Dolichonyx oryzivorus (Linnaeus). Bobolink. Resident in northern Idaho.

Burleigh (1923:655) states that the bird is resident at Clark's Fork, Bonner County.

Sturnella neglecta Audubon. Western Meadowlark. Common resident. (D. A. 1876, Boise, Ada County, May 12, 1943.)

Xanthocephalus xanthocephalus (Bonaparte). Yellow-headed Blackbird. Common resident along the Snake River in southern Idaho. (D. A. 1628, Hagerman, on Snake River, Gooding County, June 16, 1940.)

Agelaius phoeniceus (Linnaeus). Red-wing. Common resident.

a. *fortis* Ridgway. Thick-billed Red-wing. Resident in southeastern Idaho. (D. A. 1624, Hagerman on Snake River, Gooding County, June 16, 1940.)

b. *nevadensis* Grinnell. Nevada Red-wing. Resident in southwestern and northern Idaho. (D. A. 1765, Star, Canyon County, May 1, 1941.)

Icterus bullockii bullockii (Swainson). Bullock Oriole. Common resident. (D. A. 1655, 4 mi. NW Pollock, Idaho County, June 27, 1940.)

Euphagus cyanocephalus (Wagler). Brewer Blackbird. Common resident. (D. A. 1894, nest and four eggs, Boise, Ada County, May 10, 1944.)

Molothrus ater artemisiae Grinnell. Nevada Cowbird. Fairly common bird in the Upper Sonoran Life-zone. (D. A. 1460, 4-1/2 mi. SW Moscow, Latah County, May 26, 1939.)

Piranga ludoviciana (Wilson). Western Tanager. Very common resident in the Transition Life-zone. (D. A. 1570, 10 mi. ESE Moscow, Latah County, May 19, 1940.)

Pheucticus melanocephalus melanocephalus (Swainson). Rocky Mountain Grosbeak. Resident in the Transition Life-zone. (Univ. Idaho No. 51 Moscow Mountain, Latah County, May 30, 1937.)

Passerina amoena (Say). Lazuli Bunting. Very common resident in the Upper Sonoran Life-zone. (D. A. 1802, Cinch Creek, Arrowrock Reservoir, Boise County, June 28, 1941.)

Hesperiphona vespertina brooksi Grinnell. Western Evening Grosbeak. Resident in the Transition Life-zone; large flocks of these birds are commonly observed in winter. (D. A. 1527, 10 mi. ESE Moscow, Latah County, April 20, 1940.)

Carpodacus cassinii Baird. Cassin Purple Finch. Common resident in the

Transition Life-zone. (D. A. 1822, Head Crooked River, Sawtooth Range, Boise County, August 6, 1941.)

Carpodacus mexicanus solitudinis Moore. Desert House Finch. Common resident. (D. A. 1889, Boise, Ada County, April 24, 1944.)

Pinicola enucleator montana Ridgway. Rocky Mountain Pine Grosbeak. Resident on the boreal summits of the mountains. (D. A. 1321, Moscow Mountain, Latah County, January 26, 1939.)

Leucosticte tephrocotis Swainson. Rosy Finch. Resident in the boreal zones; observed casually in winter. Various races of this species are present in the State, but only the following two are here listed until there is further clarification of the status of the other races of the species.

a. *littoralis* Baird. Hepburn Rosy Finch. Winter visitant. (D. A. 1347, 2 mi. N Moscow, Latah County, March 18, 1939.)

b. *tephrocotis* (Swainson). Gray-crowned Rosy Finch. According to the 1931 A. O. U. Check-list, this subspecies breeds in the State.

Leucosticte atrata Ridgway. Black Rosy Finch. Resident in the Salmon Mountains. See A. O. U. Check-list (1931) for the range of this species.

Acanthis flammea flammea (Linnaeus). Common Redpoll. Rust (1915:127) lists this bird as a winter visitant in Kootenai County, and one specimen was obtained in Bonner County. (D. A. 1334, 6 mi. S Coolin, Bonner County, February 19, 1939.)

Spinus pinus vagrans Aldrich. Western Pine Siskin. Common resident in the Transition Life-zone. (D. A. 1857, Horseshoe Bend, Boise County, December 10, 1941.)

Spinus tristis pallidus Mearns. Pale Goldfinch. Common resident. (D. A. 1622, 4 mi. ESE Boise, Ada County, March 14, 1941.)

Loxia curvirostra Linnaeus. Red Crossbill. Uncommon resident in the Canadian Life-zone.

a. *bendirei* Ridgway. Bendire Crossbill. Resident. (D. A. 1525, 10 mi. ESE Moscow, Latah County, April 20, 1940.)

b. *benti* Griscom. Bent Crossbill. Winter visitant. (Univ. Idaho No. 94, Moscow, Latah County, December 5, 1937.)

Loxia leucoptera leucoptera Gmelin. White-winged Crossbill. Davis (1935b:236) records this bird from the Minidoka Project on December 18,

1919, and Jewett (1912b:193) took one specimen in the Sawtooth Mountains.

Chlorura chlorura (Audubon). Green-tailed Towhee. Breeding individuals of this species have been taken at the Minidoka Project by Davis (1930:136).

Pipilo maculatus Swainson. Spotted Towhee. Common resident in the Transition Life-zone.

a. *arcticus* (Swainson). Arctic Towhee. Resident in northern Idaho. (Univ. Idaho No. 163, Coeur d'Alene, Kootenai County, July 20, 1938.)

b. *curtatus* Grinnell. Nevada Towhee. Resident in southern Idaho. (D. A. 1804, Dutch Creek and Boise River, Boise County, July 4, 1941.)

Calamospiza melanocorys Stejneger. Lark Bunting. Davis (1935b:236) records this species as erratic at the Minidoka Project, where he took a specimen on May 29, 1921.

Passerculus sandwichensis nevadensis Grinnell. Nevada Savannah Sparrow. Common resident. (Univ. Idaho No. 57, Moscow, Latah County, September 25, 1937.)

Pooecetes gramineus confinis Baird. Western Vesper Sparrow. Common resident. (D. A. 1391, Moscow, Latah County, April 16, 1939.)

Chondestes grammacus strigatus Swainson. Western Lark Sparrow. Common resident. (D. A. 1579, 3 mi. SW Moscow, Latah County, May 21, 1940.)

Amphispiza belli nevadensis (Ridgway). Northern Sage Sparrow. Resident in southern Idaho. Davis (1935b:236) took one specimen in Minidoka on May 19, 1921.

Junco hyemalis cismontanus Dwight. Slate-colored Junco. Fairly common winter visitant with other juncos. See Miller (1941:329) for records of these birds.

Junco oreganus Townsend. Oregon Junco. Common resident. See Miller (1941:238) for ranges of the following subspecies.

a. *mearnsi* Ridgway. Pink-sided Junco. Resident in Custer and Fremont counties.

b. *montanus* Ridgway. Montana Junco. Resident in northern and western Idaho.

Junco caniceps caniceps (Woodhouse). Gray-headed Junco. Miller

(1941:180) states that some hybridization occurs between this species and *oreganus* in Bannock and Cassia counties. It is resident in southeastern Idaho.

Spizella arborea ochracea Brewster. Western Tree Sparrow. Fairly common resident in central and northern Idaho. (D. A. 1516, nest and eggs, Moscow, Latah County, April 6, 1940.)

Spizella passerina arizonae Coues. Western Chipping Sparrow. Very common resident in the Transition Life-zone. (D. A. 1805, junction of Dutch Creek and Boise River, Boise County, July 4, 1941.)

Spizella breweri breweri Cassin. Brewer Sparrow. Resident in southern Idaho. Davis (1935b:235) records the bird as a summer resident at the Minidoka Project.

Zonotrichia querula Nuttall. Harris Sparrow. Wyman (1911a:267) records this bird from Nampa, Valley County, in winter.

Zonotrichia leucophrys (Forster). White-crowned Sparrow. Common resident.

a. *gambeli* (Nuttall). Gambel Sparrow. Migrant. (Univ. Idaho No. 6, Moscow, Latah County, September 26, 1936.)

b. *leucophrys* (Forster). White-crowned Sparrow. Resident in the Hudsonian and Canadian zones. See A. O. U. Check-list (1931) for range of this subspecies.

Zonotrichia albicollis (Gmelin). White-throated Sparrow. Wyman (1912b:247) reported this bird from Nampa, Valley County, in winter.

Passerella iliaca schistacea Baird. Slate-colored Fox Sparrow. Uncommon resident in the Transition Life-zone, and fairly common in migration. (D. A. 1365, Pocatello Creek, 3 mi. E Pocatello, Bannock County, April 2, 1939.)

Melospiza lincolnii alticola (Miller and McCabe). Montane Lincoln Sparrow. Resident in the boreal zones, and fairly common in migration. See Miller and McCabe (1935:149) for range of this subspecies.

Melospiza melodia (Wilson). Song Sparrow. Common resident.

a. *fallax* (Baird). Mountain Song Sparrow. Resident in southern Idaho. (D. A. 1839, Head Taylor Creek, Boise County, August 7, 1941.)

b. *merrilli* Brewster. Merrill Song Sparrow. Resident in central and northern Idaho. (Univ. Idaho No. 103, Moscow, Latah County, February 22, 1938.)

Calcarius lapponicus alascensis Ridgway. Alaska Longspur. Uncommon migrant. Merrill (1898:15) records one specimen of this species taken at Fort Sherman on November 13, 1896.

Plectrophenax nivalis nivalis (Linnaeus). Eastern Snow Bunting. Uncommon migrant. Rust (1915:127) records the bird as rare in migration in Kootenai County, and Merrill (1898:15) states that it is irregular in winter at Fort Sherman.

BIBLIOGRAPHY

Aldrich, J. W.

1944. Notes on the races of the white-breasted nuthatch. Auk, 61:592-604.

1946a. New subspecies of birds from western North America. Proc. Biol. Soc. Washington, 59:129-136.

1946b. Speciation in the white-cheeked geese. Wilson Bull., 58:94-103.

Aldrich, J. W. and Friedmann, H.

1943. A revision of the ruffed grouse. Condor, 45:85-103.

American Ornithologists' Union Committee.

1931. Check-list of North American birds. Lancaster Press.

1944. Nineteenth supplement to the American Ornithologists' Union check-list of North American birds. Auk, 61:441-464.

1945. Twentieth supplement to the American Ornithologists' Union check-list of North American birds. Auk, 62:436-449.

1946. Twenty-first supplement to the American Ornithologists' Union check-list of North American birds. Auk, 63:428-432.

1947. Twenty-second supplement to the American Ornithologists' Union check-list of North American birds. Auk, 64:445-452.

Arvey, M. D.

1941. Black-billed cuckoo in Idaho. Condor, 43:291.

1944. Eastern blue-jay in Idaho. Condor, 46:205.

Behle, W. H.

1942. Distribution and variation of the horned larks (*Otocoris alpestris*) of western North America. Univ. California Publ. Zoöl., 46:205-316.

1944. Check-list of the birds of Utah. Condor, 46:67-87.

Bendire, C. E.

1877. Birds of southeastern Oregon. Proc. Boston Soc. Nat. Hist., 19:109-149.

Bond, R. M.

1946. The peregrine population of western North America. Condor,

48:101-116.

Brewster, W.

1896. Description of a new warbler and a new song sparrow. Auk, 13:44-47.

Brodkorb, P.

1935a. Two new subspecies of the red-shafted flicker. Occ. Pap. Mus. Zoöl., Univ. Michigan, 314:1-3.

1935b. A new bird for Idaho. Auk, 52:312.

Burleigh, T. D.

1923. Notes on the breeding birds of Clark's Fork, Bonner County, Idaho, Auk, 40:653-665.

Coole, H. K.

1915. The present status of the trumpeter swan (*Olor buccinator*). Auk, 32:82-90.

Coues, E.

1892. Original description of Lewis's woodpecker. Auk, 9:394.

Davis, W. B.

1923. On the avifauna of Minidoka County, and adjacent territory. Murrelet, 4:3-4.

1930. Meet *Oreospiza chlorura*. Oologist, 47:136.

1934. Bird notes from Owyhee County, Idaho. Murrelet, 15:69-72.

1935a. Noon-day feeding of the Pacific nighthawk. Condor, 37:176.

1935b. An analysis of the bird population in the vicinity of Rupert, Idaho. Condor, 37:233-238.

1936. Broad-winged hawk in Idaho. Condor, 38:86.

Davis, W. B. and Stevenson, J.

1934. The type localities of three birds collected by Lewis and Clark in 1806. Condor, 36:161-163.

Duvall, H. J.

1945. Distribution and taxonomy of the black-capped chickadees of North America. Auk, 62:49-69.

Evendon, F. G., Jr., and Evendon, J. R.

1944. A house finch census at Mountain Home, Idaho. Condor,

46:209.

Grinnell, J.

1904. The origin and distribution of the chestnut-backed chickadee. Auk, 21:364-382.

Hand, R. L.

1933a. The hawk-owl in northern Idaho. Condor, 35:32.

1933b. Summer occurrence of the goshawk in Idaho. Condor, 35:36.

1935. A sight record of the red phalarope (*P. fulicans*) in northern Idaho. Auk, 52:180-181.

1938. Notes on some birds nesting in northern Idaho. Condor, 41:84.

Hayward, C. L.

1934. Important heron rookeries in southeastern Idaho. Auk, 51:39-41.

Hurley, J. B.

1926. Birds observed in Idaho, Washington, and Oregon. Murrelet, 7:35-36.

Jewett, S. G.

1912a. Western records of the catbird. Auk, 29:106.

1912b. Some birds of the Sawtooth Mountains, Idaho. Condor, 14:191-194.

Jones, V. E.

1943. White-fronted goose in Idaho. Condor, 45:120.

1946. The starling in Idaho. Condor, 48:142-143.

Kenagy, F.

1914. A change in fauna. Condor, 16:120-123.

Low, J. B.

1945. Clay bank has multiple use for wildlife. Condor, 47:132-133.

Low, J. B., and Nelson, M.

1945. Recent records of breeding waterfowl in Utah and southern Idaho. Condor, 47:131-132.

Marshall, W. H.

1940. An "Eagle Guard" developed in Idaho. Condor, 52:166.

McCabe, T. T., and McCabe, E. B.

1933. Hermit thrushes of the northwestern states. Condor, 35:122-123.

Merriam, C. H.

1891. Results of a biological reconnaisance of south-central Idaho. N. Amer. Fauna, 5:1-108.

1892. The dwarf screech owl (*Megascops flammeolus idahoensis* Merriam). Auk, 9:169-171.

Merrill, J. C.

1897. Notes on the birds of Fort Sherman, Idaho. Auk, 14:347-357.

1898. Notes on the birds of Fort Sherman, Idaho. Auk, 15:14-22.

Miller, A. H.

1931. Systematic revision and natural history of the American shrikes (*Lanius*). Univ. California Publ. Zoöl., 38:11-242.

1933. The Canada jays of northern Idaho. Trans. San Diego Soc. Nat. Hist., 7:287-296.

1941. Speciation in the avian genus *Junco*. Univ. California Publ. Zoöl., 44:173-434.

Miller, A. H. and McCabe, T. T.

1935. Racial differentiation in *Passerella (Melospiza) lincolnii*. Condor, 37:144-160.

Moore, R. T.

1939. A review of the house finches of the subgenus Burrica. Condor, 41:177-205.

Oberholser, H. C.

1918. Notes on the subspecies of *Numenius americanus* Bechstein. Auk, 35:188-195.

Olson, A. C., Jr.

1943. Starling in northern Idaho. Condor, 45:197.

Palmer, R. H.

1928. Relative abundance of bird species in southern Idaho, Fresno County, California, and King County, Washington. Murrelet, 9:28-38.

Ridgway, R.

1901-1918. The birds of North and Middle America. U. S. Nat. Mus. Bull. 50, pts. 1-8.

Rust, H. J.

1913. Birds new to the vicinity of Lake Coeur d'Alene, Kootenai County, Idaho. Condor, 15:41.

1914. Some notes on the nesting of the sharp-shinned hawk. Condor, 16:14-24.

1915. An annotated list of the birds of Kootenai County, Idaho. Condor, 17:118-129.

1916. Additional notes on the birds of Kootenai County, Idaho. Condor, 18:81-82.

1917. An annotated list of the birds of Fremont County, Idaho, as observed during the summer of 1916. Condor, 19:29-43.

1919. A favorite nesting haunt of the Merrill song sparrow. Condor, 21:145-153.

1920. The home life of the western warbling vireo. Condor, 22:85-94.

Slipp, J. W.

1942. Franklin's gull in Idaho. Condor, 44:226-227.

Sloanaker, J. L.

1925. Notes from Spokane. Condor, 27:73-74.

Snyder, J. O.

1900. Notes on a few species of Idaho and Washington birds. Auk, 17:242-245.

Stone, W.

1915. Type locality of Lewis's woodpecker and Clarke's nutcracker. Auk, 32:371-372.

Sugden, J. W.

1937. The status of the sandhill crane in Utah and southern Idaho. Condor, 40:18-22.

Taverner, P. A.

1914. A new subspecies of *Dendragapus* (*Dendragapus obscurus flemmingi*) from southern Yukon Territory. Auk, 31:385-388.

Taylor, W. P.

1918. Bohemian waxwing (*Bombycilla garrula*) breeding within the United States. Auk, 35:226-227.

Tracy, H. C.

1910. The bobolink in Idaho. Condor, 12:80.

van Rossem, A. J.

1929. A northern race of the mountain chickadee. Auk, 45:104-105.

Wyman, L. E.

1911a. Harris's sparrow (*Zonotrichia querula*) in southern Idaho. Auk, 28:267-268.

1911b. The bobolink again in Idaho. Condor, 13:75.

1911c. The catbird in southern Idaho. Condor, 13:108.

1912a. Bobolink again in Idaho. Condor, 14:41.

1912b. White-throated sparrow in Idaho. Auk, 29:247.

1912c. *Oreortyx* in Idaho. Auk, 29:538-539.

Transmitted February 12, 1947.

21-6960